Bangladesh

Bangladesh

BY TAMRA B. ORR

Enchantment of the World
Second Series

Children's Press®

A Division of Scholastic Inc.

NEW YORK TORONTO LONDON AUCKLAND SYDNEY
MEXICO CITY NEW DELHI HONG KONG
DANBURY, CONNECTICUT

Frontispiece: Mangrove forest along the southwestern coast

Consultant: Richard B. Barnett, Corcoran Department of History, University of Virginia, Charlottesville, Virginia

Please note: All statistics are as up-to-date as possible at the time of publication.

Book production by Herman Adler

Library of Congress Cataloging-in-Publication Data

Orr, Tamra.
  Bangladesh / by Tamra Orr.
      p. cm. — (Enchantment of the world. Second series)
  Includes bibliographical references and index.
  ISBN-13: 978-0-516-25012-0
  ISBN-10: 0-516-25012-4
  1. Bangladesh—Juvenile literature. I. Title. II. Series.
  DS393.4.O77 2007
  954.92—dc22   2006024160

Bangladesh

Cover photo:
Young woman talking
on a cell phone

Contents

Harvesting crops

Terra-cotta pots

To Save
a Tiger

T

ODAY, I AM IN DHAKA. I HEARD MANY STORIES ABOUT this city when I was a child, but not one compares with the reality. It is busy, loud, and exciting. I am always glad to come to the city, but I know that by the time my work here is over, it will be a relief to return to my quiet village.

I am here in Dhaka on an important mission. I am here to help save the tigers—the powerful symbol of my country.

Opposite: **Royal Bengal tigers, which can weigh up to 660 pounds (300 kilograms), were once common, but are now endangered.**

People, bicycles, and rickshaws crowd the streets of Dhaka.

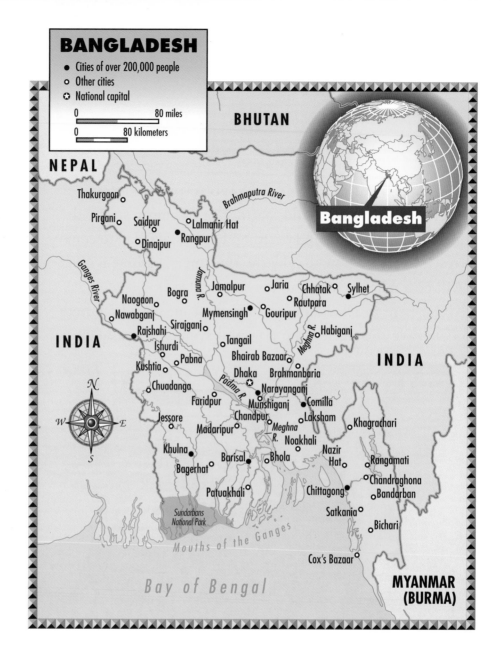

The Royal Bengal tigers represent such pride and grace, I am honored to be a part of trying to save them. A hundred years ago, forty thousand tigers lived in South Asia. By the 1970s, their population had dropped to just two thousand. They

became endangered. As a child, I heard this and was saddened. As fierce and dangerous as these animals can be, they are also sleek and graceful. They deserve to live their lives in the country that we share.

When I think of the tigers, I cannot separate their history from mine. As a child, I listened to stories of their bravery and spirit. As an adult, I am working to keep them safe.

Bangladesh is my home. Unlike many people in my country, I had the chance to go to school and get a college degree. Since my work with the Save the Tiger Foundation began a decade ago, I have traveled to other parts of the world. Now, whenever I come back to Bangladesh, I see my homeland through new eyes. It is such a beautiful place, but it has such great problems.

A Royal Bengal tiger relaxes in a mangrove forest in the Sundarbans.

Rickshaws are a quick and popular means of transportation in Bangladeshi cities.

There are people everywhere. Here in Dhaka, it is hard to even move from one place to another. Bangladesh is the world's eighth most populated country. China and India have more people, but they also have much more land. Other countries I have been to seem empty in comparison.

When I arrived in Dhaka this morning, I was taken to my hotel in a bicycle rickshaw. Many of my cousins own rickshaws. They are very proud of them. This one had a beautiful carriage with streamers and some plastic flowers on each side of the seat. The driver was strong and fearless. He stood up on the pedals, and it felt as if we were flying. He threaded his way through the traffic without hesitation. I kept closing my eyes and hoping I wouldn't find myself spilled onto the ground.

Bangladesh is the last real home of the Royal Bengal tiger. People from all over the world are coming to a conference in

Dhaka to evaluate which programs have been most effective in protecting them. We will discuss ways of convincing the people who live near the great beasts that it is in their interest to protect them. The tigers face a serious threat here in Bangladesh. How can people live alongside such a ferocious animal and survive? How can tigers live next to people, when there is so little room that they cannot help but get in each other's way? I don't have all the answers, but I must try to make a difference if I can.

The stripes on Royal Bengal tigers are like fingerprints. No two animals have the same pattern.

Today, I took a ride on a "country boat." I have often watched these boats as they have taken cargo from one place to another. In Bangladesh, there are more waterways than there are paved roads, so boats are the most efficient way of getting around. Fortunately, our boat was going with the current. This makes for a fast, smooth trip. The crew raised the sails and caught the wind. They said that on the journey back, they would not be as lucky. They would have to use poles and muscle to push the boat through the water.

The river was full of all kinds of water traffic. I saw large ferries and small paddleboats. During our trip, we passed a paddle wheeler. I knew it was on its regular route from Dhaka to

Paddle wheelers are called "rockets" in Bangladesh. They are often the best way to travel around the country.

Khulna. I have ridden it often with my friends and family. As usual, it was completely full—almost overflowing on all sides with people. I also saw a group of houseboats with entire families on them. Small children ran around the deck, playing and shouting. These were the *bede* people. They spend their entire lives on the water. Some of them sell herbal potions or the pink pearls they have harvested from river oysters. What would it be like to grow up with the water underneath me instead of the ground?

Boats of all types, from canoes to steamers, carry passengers and cargo across the country's many rivers, lakes, and swamps.

May 17

The days have been so full that there is little free time to sit down and write. We are working as hard as we can to finish our conference and send the foreigners back home before the monsoon season begins in June. The weather has been hot and damp. I watch the Americans as they change clothes three times a day to try to stay dry. I am used to this heat,

Bangladesh is a low-lying country with more than seven hundred rivers. Flooding is common during the monsoon season.

and I know that as uncomfortable as it is now, it will be much worse when the rainy season begins. I have lost count of how many terrible storms I have survived. I sometimes fear the powerful thunderstorms, torrential rain, punishing winds, and tidal waves.

Tonight, a group of us from the foundation are having dinner with my sister's family. I am looking forward to the traditional tea and rice, as I sometimes miss them when I am abroad. We Bangladeshis eat rice often, even in desserts. Rice fields are everywhere. I hope we have *chapattis* tonight, too. It is sometimes hard to find such good, tasty breads when I am in other countries.

Time is growing tight. We met with a number of Bangladeshis today and talked about how to solve the problem of tigers attacking people. The tigers have lost their habitat, and they have been hunted by poachers who want to sell their strikingly colored coats. There are laws in place to protect these magnificent animals, but they are often ignored. I can understand why. The Royal Bengal tiger will attack any person in its path, and people have little choice but to protect themselves. One of our biggest frustrations is that many of my people rely solely on prayer for protection from these huge animals. I myself have many times prayed for safety as I or someone in my family has headed out into an area where tigers live.

People at the foundation do not want to discourage religious beliefs. But they

Since 1973, it has been illegal to hunt or injure Royal Bengal tigers.

are trying to teach people to carry big sticks or take along guard dogs that can warn of a tiger's presence. These are good ideas, and I hope I can help convince the people to think about them.

May 29

It is time for the other people from the foundation to head back home. The weather is beginning to look threatening. This land is already so full of water, the foreigners cannot imagine what it is like when the rains come. The entire landscape changes. New pathways are created and old ones disappear under the water, almost overnight.

I will make a full report at the meeting tomorrow on the state of our efforts to work with local people to protect the tiger. And then it will be time to head back to my village for a visit with my family.

I enjoy working with foreigners and introducing them to my country. My mind is full of pride for my country and its people. We have tremendous poverty, but we also have incredible kindness. The tigers that live so near to where I sit right now are breathtakingly beautiful and graceful. I feel honored to be part of the system that is trying to save them. I feel even more honored to call myself a Bangladeshi.

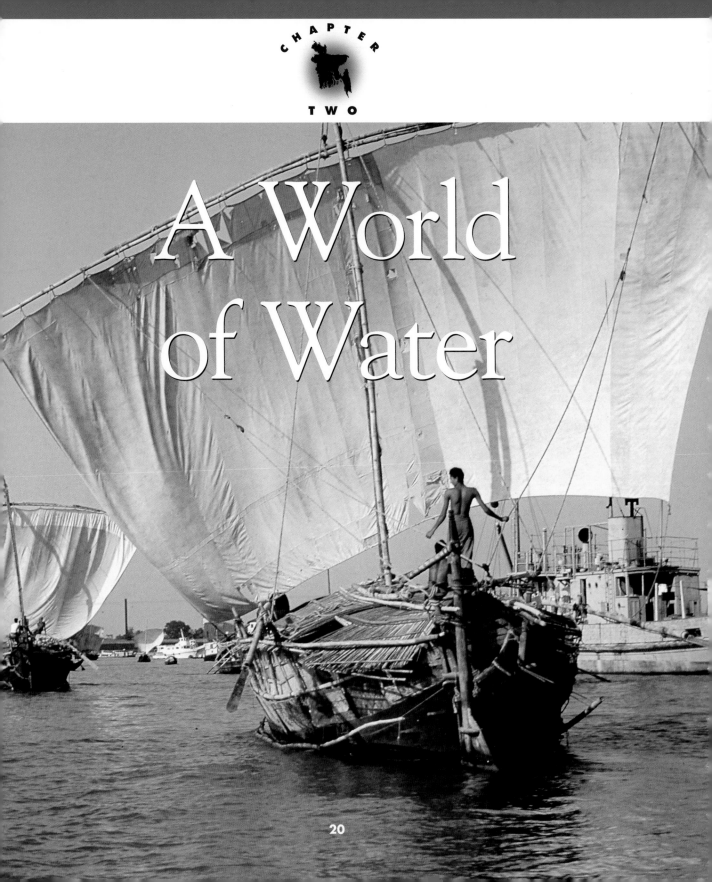

A World
of Water

Finding Bangladesh on a world map can be a little challenging. Despite its enormous population, it is a tiny country, measuring just 55,584 square miles (143,962 square kilometers). That's a bit smaller than the state of Iowa. The easiest way to find Bangladesh is to search first for India, in South Asia. Then look to the east and you will see Bangladesh. India borders Bangladesh on the west, north, and east, while a bit of Myanmar (formerly known as Burma) is to the southeast. The Bay of Bengal lies to the south. Bangladesh is part of a region known as Bengal. In fact, it is sometimes called East Bengal. West Bengal is a state in India.

Opposite: **Jute, Bangladesh's major export, grows underwater and is often transported by boat.**

Several rivers cross the border between Bangladesh and India, which is 2,518 miles (4,053 km) long.

Nearly all of Bangladesh is made up of flat land called alluvial plains. For eons, rivers flooded and left behind deposits of dirt and rock. These deposits formed the alluvial plains, which are extremely fertile.

Most of Bangladesh's alluvial plains are less than 50 feet (15 meters) above sea level. The country's only hilly areas are in the northeast and southeast. In the northeast are the low hills of Sylhet, rolling hills that are covered with tea plantations and rain forests. The country's highest elevation is 4,035 feet (1,230 m), at Mount Keokradong in the southeastern Chittagong Hills.

Most of Bangladesh is low and flat. Crops grow well in the rich soil.

Bangladesh's Geographic Features

Area: 55,584 square miles (143,962 sq km)

Greatest Distance East to West: 410 miles (660 km)

Greatest Distance North to South: 509 miles (820 km)

Longest Shared Border: 2,518 miles (4,053 km), with India

Length of Coastline: 360 miles (580 km)

Highest Elevation: Mount Keokradong, 4,035 feet (1,230 m)

Lowest Elevation: Sea level, along the Indian Ocean

Longest River: Surma-Meghna river system, 434 miles (699 km) long

Highest Average Rainfall: 235 inches (596 cm) in the northeast

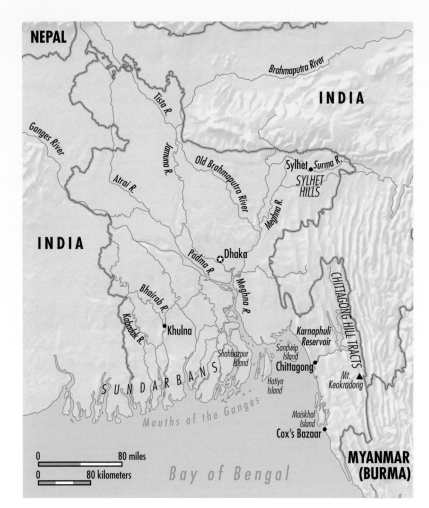

Scattered over the plains are three large cities and more than sixty thousand small villages. Three-quarters of Bangladeshis live in rural areas in simple homes without running water or electricity. Most city dwellers live in slum areas called *bustees*.

Bangladeshis sometimes harvest crops, such as rice and hyacinths, by boat.

Water, Water Everywhere

Water defines the Bangladeshi landscape. The country has about 5,000 miles (8,000 km) of waterways. Everywhere you go, there are rivers, lakes, swamps, and marshes—and that is in the dry season. More than seven hundred rivers cut through Bangladesh. The Ganges enters in the west and flows southeast. The Brahmaputra, which flows from India in the north, is called the Jamuna in Bangladesh. It joins the Ganges near Dhaka, where they become the Padma. The Surma becomes the Meghna soon after it crosses the border in the northeast. It, too, meets up with the Padma. Eventually, all of Bangladesh's rivers flow into the Bay of Bengal in the south. In many places, small waterways split off from a large river and make their way across the soggy land in all directions.

The paths water takes across the ground change with the amount of rainfall and flooding. When an old channel dries up, it often leaves a raised area called a *char*. Since land is scarce in Bangladesh, families sometimes settle on one of these small islands. They try to plant crops before the water rises again and washes everything away. Although living on chars is illegal, some people are willing to risk getting caught in the hopes of having a home and growing food.

Bangladesh's main rivers divide the country into plains and deltas—the sandy, muddy spots left by rivers passing through. In the southwest, where rivers overflow regularly, there is a

Bangladeshi boys play on Dhal Char near the Bay of Bengal.

huge, marshy forest called the Sundarbans. Covering 540 square miles (1,400 sq km), the Sundarbans—whose name means "beautiful forest"—is lovely.

The Sundarbans stretches along the Bay of Bengal from the delta of the Meghna River in Bangladesh to the delta of the Hooghly River in India. Lining the coast is the largest mangrove forest in the world. Mangroves are trees that are able to grow up out of the salt water. These unusual trees provide timber and firewood, but more importantly, they are a buffer between the sea's high storm waves and the Bangladeshi people. The Sundarbans is the least-populated section of Bangladesh. But many fishermen, woodcutters, and honey gatherers come to the Sundarbans to find food as well as valuable materials like leaves for roofing and grass for matting. Hunting is not permitted in the area.

Unlike most trees, mangroves grow in salt water. Many have roots that block salt from entering the tree.

Looking at Bangladesh's Cities

Chittagong is the second-largest city in Bangladesh, with 5 million people. It lies in a beautiful part of the southeast, surrounded by a bay, a river, and hills. A port city, Chittagong is the commercial and manufacturing center for Bangladesh. Chittagong has many interesting sights. The Shrine of Bayazid Bostami has a pond filled with hundreds of turtles thought to be the descendants of evil spirits. The huge Chittagong Court Building (right) was built by the British in the 1800s. Foy's Lake, an artificial waterway, is a perfect spot for picnickers.

The city of Khulna (below) in the southwest is home to 2.4 million people. Khulna is an industrial city where many ships are built. It is also the site of a naval base and of the nation's telephone and cable companies.

Kaptai Lake, in the Chittagong Hill Tracts, was created when the Karnaphuli River was dammed.

Hills and an Island

Two of the country's most interesting areas are the Chittagong Hill Tracts and Hatiya Island. They stand out because they are so unlike the flat land that makes up most of Bangladesh.

The Chittagong Hill Tracts in the southeast are completely different from the rest of Bangladesh. The nation's only mountains are found in this region. It is also home to one of Bangladesh's last major forests, where wildlife can roam free.

Hatiya Island sits in the Bay of Bengal, two hours by boat from the mainland. It is only 25 miles (40 km) long and 9 miles (14 km) wide, yet somehow three hundred thousand people live there. Hatiya Island has only one road and no hospital or medical center. Houses sit on raised platforms to prevent them from being washed out by high storm tides. Cyclones are a frequent danger, and in 1991, a tidal wave devastated the island, wiping out 90 percent of the houses.

Beach, Beach, and More Beach

Beach lovers will think they have found heaven if they visit the city of Cox's Bazaar along the southeastern coast. It claims to have the longest natural beach in the world. Cox's Bazaar is the tourist capital of Bangladesh because it offers a little of everything: 75 miles (120 km) of golden sand, high cliffs, pounding surf, rare shells, Buddhist temples, elegant pagodas, and tasty seafood. Visitors admire the thundering waterfalls, remote monasteries, and a bronze statue of the Buddha that stands 13 feet (4 m) tall.

Trouble in the Air and Water

It is no surprise that a small country bursting with people suffers from water and air pollution. Large cities like Dhaka have some of the worst air quality in the world. A staggering number of old and badly maintained buses, cars, and trucks emitting pollutants clog Dhaka's streets. During a traffic jam, the air is gray and stagnant, full of exhaust chemicals.

In 2000, the Bangladesh Air Quality Management Project was founded. It has been working to teach mechanics and car owners how to keep their vehicles in better condition so they don't produce as much pollution.

Water pollution is also a problem in Bangladesh. Finding clean drinking water is difficult. The water often contains poisons or germs that produce diseases such as diarrhea, hepatitis, and typhoid fever.

Air pollution is a serious problem in Dhaka, Chittagong, Khulna, and Rajshahi, the four major cities in Bangladesh.

Deadly Weather

Monsoon season is an annual danger for the people of Bangladesh. Because of the country's unusually flat land and many waterways, it is slammed far worse than other countries. As the monsoon winds pick up to more than 100 miles per hour (160 kph), rain and ocean water batter the land. Cities are flooded, crops are lost, people are killed, and homes are destroyed. Rivers that are already full merge with the storm waters and overflow. Even after the waters begin to recede, they are still dangerous. They often carry germs of deadly diseases like cholera and typhoid.

Bangladesh has also suffered many devastating cyclones. In 1970, the Bhola Cyclone killed at least 500,000 people. The 1991 Bangladesh Cyclone produced a 20-foot (6 m) wall of water that killed 139,000 people and left more than 10 million homeless.

In recent years, the Bangladesh government has tried to prepare for future disasters by building more than 2,500 elevated cyclone shelters and training people in search-and-rescue methods. Hopefully, the next major storm to hit will not be as devastating.

But many scientists fear that the storms and flooding will only grow worse in the coming years. Scientists have found that the average temperatures on Earth are increasing. As this global warming melts glaciers and the polar ice caps, ocean levels will rise. Since most of Bangladesh sits only 30 feet (10 m) above sea level, rising ocean levels are a particular threat. If the waters were to rise just 3 feet (1 m), about 10 percent of Bangladesh would be under water.

UNICEF, an international organization that promotes children's health, helped the country drill several million wells in order to find clean water. This seemed like the perfect solution. Unfortunately, it was later discovered that at least half of these wells were contaminated with arsenic, a deadly chemical. The arsenic seems to occur naturally in the earth under Bangladesh. Now, many families have to repeatedly test their wells for arsenic.

Clean water is one of the most hard to come by commodities in Bangladesh.

Hot, Humid, and Wet

People in Bangladesh live with year-round heat and humidity. The country has three basic seasons: winter (October to March), summer (March to June), and monsoon (June to October). Summer is usually humid, with temperatures reaching an average high of 92 degrees Fahrenheit (33 degrees Celsius). Daily afternoon thunderstorms are typical, as are occasional hailstorms. Winter is slightly cooler, but temperatures still usually rise to at least 80°F (27°C) every day and rarely fall below 45°F (7°C).

Monsoon season is the most trying time in Bangladesh. Monsoons are strong winds that bring warm, wet air from the Indian Ocean. During monsoon season, temperatures often reach 100°F (38°C), and it rains all the time. In fact, 80 percent of the country's annual rainfall arrives during monsoon season—and that's a lot of water. Bangladesh is one of the rainiest places in the world. The west receives 55 inches (140 centimeters) per year, while the soggy northeast averages about 235 inches (600 cm) per year.

To make matters worse, monsoon season is also cyclone season. Cyclones are powerful storms that form over the ocean. They often crash into Bangladesh, bringing devastation and death. As cyclones batter the country, rivers swell and run over their banks. Waterways change course, crops are ruined, and people do their best to survive and keep going. Life is a struggle for people, plants, and animals.

The combination of monsoon winds and strong storms regularly causes flooding in Bangladesh.

Bursting
with Color

Lush grasses blanket a riverbank.

BANGLADESH'S RICH SOIL AND PLENTIFUL WATER ALLOW plants, flowers, and animals to thrive. The land is bursting with varied and colorful life.

Nature's Paradise

Bangladesh is a fruit lover's paradise. Mangoes, bananas, pineapples, watermelons, guavas, and coconuts grow there. Flowers such as orchids, marigolds, lotus, and jasmine abound in Bangladesh's wet land. The bright red-orange petals of flame-of-the-forest and the blue petals and thick green leaves of water hyacinth are common sights. Floating ferns are found in floodplains, and tall grasses grace many riverbanks. Houses are often hidden among bamboo thickets and banana trees.

Opposite: **In the wild, Asiatic elephants live for an average of sixty years.**

The Giant Jackfruit

The jackfruit is Bangladesh's national fruit. It can grow to weigh 110 pounds (50 kg)—no other tree fruit grows as large. The jackfruit looks like a fuzzy green fur ball from another planet. Bangladeshis love its unique flavor, which is like a mix of banana and pineapple. The jackfruit is quite seedy, with up to five hundred seeds in each section. Seeds are often roasted or fried and then eaten.

About 15 percent of Bangladesh is forested. The mangrove trees that line its southern coast provide shelter for sea creatures and protect against the sea's most powerful waves. Palm and tamarind trees grow throughout the country. Teak is found in the Sundarbans, and Chittagong boasts rain forests.

The warm and wet climate of Bangladesh is ideal for palm trees.

The Shapla

The *shapla* (water lily) is Bangladesh's national flower. It symbolizes the country's many rivers and is often depicted in murals and embroidered cloth. It is even part of the national emblem. The shapla blooms during the warmest months, and its strong pink or white petals are commonly seen floating on waterways.

Diverse Life

Bangladesh is home to an amazing array of creatures. More than 200 species of mammals, 750 species of birds, 150 species of reptiles and amphibians, and 200 species of fish can be found in Bangladesh.

Chital deer eat mainly grasses and fallen leaves and flowers.

Several kinds of deer live among the wooded hills in eastern and northeastern Bangladesh. The sambar deer is quite large, growing up to 5 feet (1.5 m) tall at the shoulder and weighing more than 600 pounds (270 kilograms). The chital deer is smaller. It grows to an average of 3 feet (1 m) tall and weighs 190 pounds (85 kg). The chital are lovely, with

golden brown fur that is covered in erratic, bright-white spots. They move in herds of ten to thirty through grassy forest glades and along the edges of shady streams. The smallest type of deer in Bangladesh is the barking deer. When they are scared, barking deer make a sound much like a dog's bark.

A number of ape and monkey species live in the Sundarbans and the Chittagong Hill Tracts. The hoolock gibbon is one of the most unusual. It is known as the "singing ape" because it defends its territory by whistling. Its eerie whistle echoes through the forest. Several hundred Asiatic elephants also live in the Chittagong Hill Tracts. Though smaller than African elephants, they are still very large. They can reach

Langur monkeys are sometimes called leaf monkeys because leaves are their primary food source.

The Royal Bengal Tiger

The Royal Bengal tiger is one of the most spectacular creatures roaming through the jungles and mangrove forests of the Sundarbans. This cat grows up to 13 feet (4 m) long and weighs up to 660 pounds (300 kg). It typically feeds on deer, antelope, and wild pigs. Since it is a good swimmer, it will also leap into the water and have a meal of lizards, turtles, or crabs.

Tigers have striking red-yellow coats with black stripes, which are coveted by people all over the world. This is one reason the tiger is now endangered. A hundred years ago, more than forty thousand of these majestic creatures prowled the forests of Bangladesh and India. But hunting and loss of habitat caused their numbers to drop to fewer than two thousand.

Finally, in 1972 and 1973, two groups called the Save the Tiger Foundation and Project Tiger were set up to help protect these animals. Reserves were established for the tigers, and hunting or injuring a tiger became illegal. These measures have slowly been producing results. Today, more than four thousand tigers live in Bangladesh.

The tigers' problems are not over, however. Unlike many big cats, the tiger is not afraid to attack a human in its path. In fact, tigers have been known to plunge right into the water and grab fishermen out of their boats. How can the Bangladeshis protect both the tigers and themselves? It is a difficult question. Some people use prayer to protect themselves. They hope that is enough to keep them safe. Others take extra precautions, such as making electrified fishing dummies. If a tiger attacks a fishing dummy, it gets a nasty shock. The men who gather honey in the forests have a different method of protecting themselves. Since the tigers attack from behind, some men have taken to wearing face masks on the back of their heads. So far, none of them have been attacked.

One bite from a king cobra delivers enough venom to kill an elephant or twenty people.

9 feet (2.7 m) at the shoulder and weigh 3.5 tons (3,200 kg). The Sundarbans is home to a number of frightening creatures, including pythons 15 feet (4.5 m) long and crocodiles that grow to three times the size of an average man.

Other creatures found in Bangladesh include the South Himalayan black bear, the Malayan black bear, and the sloth bear. Foxes, weasels, and wolves also roam the country. Tortoises, mud turtles, and king cobras live near Bangladesh's many bodies of water. Living in the water are mudskippers, gobies, shrimps, prawns, lobsters, crabs, and stingrays, as well as bull, hammerhead, tiger, and sandbar sharks.

On the Wing

The skies over Bangladesh are often filled with a riot of color and songs. The mynah bird has a yellow bill and yellow legs, dark red and black feathers, and a splash of white on the end of its wings. They can often be spotted sitting on the back of cattle or perched in a tree. More than twenty types of woodpecker can be heard rat-a-tat-tatting in Bangladesh, while a dozen varieties of kingfisher fly around.

In the Sylhet region, there is a lowland area known as the *haors*. In the winter, huge flocks of fowl settle there, especially Baer's pochard and the Pallas's fish-eagle. In the forests, blue-bearded bee eaters and redheaded trogons live in

A flameback woodpecker searches for food in the Sundarbans. Insects are their main food.

The Mimicking Magpie

The *doel,* or magpie robin, is Bangladesh's national bird. It has blue-black feathers and splashes of white on its tail and sides. It is often seen darting in and out of the shrubbery in towns or sitting in treetops, singing. The doel is usually a shy bird, but when searching for a mate, it calls loudly, often imitating the calls of other birds. If a male magpie feels threatened by another bird, it will strut and puff out its feathers to let the strange bird know it is not welcome.

the trees, while on Hatiya Island, species such as the spoon-billed sandpiper, Nordman's greenshank, and Indian skimmers are found.

Insects Good and Bad

Four types of bees buzz around the country's flowers. They make honey from the nectar they collect. Many Bangladeshis search the forests for this sweet treat to sell at the market and perhaps share with their eager family.

Another insect found throughout Bangladesh is the mosquito. Mosquitoes thrive in places with standing water, so Bangladesh is paradise to them. But they are a major prob-

The Dhaka Zoo

The Dhaka Zoo is the largest zoo in Bangladesh. It covers 185 acres (75 hectares) and includes two lakes. That space is home to almost two hundred species of animals. Among the ninety species of birds, sixty-four species of mammals, and fifteen species of reptiles are such rare creatures as waterbucks, impalas, emus, tapirs, lions, and mandrills. Each year, more than three million visitors come to the zoo to see its many fantastic creatures.

lem for people. Besides being a bother, mosquitoes carry serious diseases like malaria, which kills thousands of Bangladeshis every year.

Protecting Wildlife

The plants and animals found in Bangladesh are impressive and beautiful. The biggest problem they face is the same one that plagues the Bangladeshi people—a lack of room and resources. Fortunately, as the number of animals drops, organizations such as the Wildlife Trust of Bangladesh, the Bangladesh Forest Department, and the Zoo Outreach Organisation have stepped in to make changes that may help prevent more species from being added to the endangered list.

A man gathers honey in the Sundarbans.

Thanks to the Bangladesh Wildlife Preservation Amendment Act of 1974, the country now has multiple wildlife sanctuaries and game reserves. These protected areas help 500 species of plants and 840 species of animals stay safer.

A New
Independence

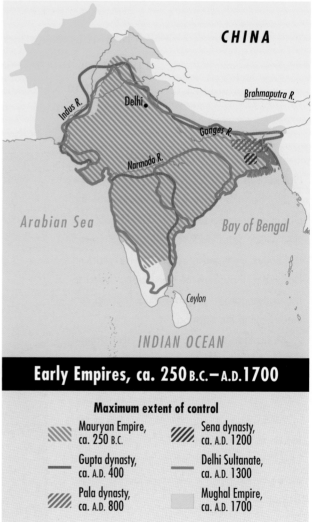

PEOPLE HAVE BEEN LIVING IN THE AREA THAT IS NOW Bangladesh for thousands of years, but the nation is quite young. It achieved independence only in 1971.

Opposite: **A gold coin depicts Kumaragupta I, who ruled in the early 400s.**

The First People

The first people to live in what is now Bangladesh were a group called the Bang. They came to the area as early as 1000 B.C. Most likely, they had been driven out of their homelands to the north.

More is known about the Mauryan Empire, which ruled the area between 273 and 232 B.C. This empire controlled all of what is now India and Pakistan, as well as parts of Iran and Afghanistan. By A.D. 320, the Gupta dynasty had taken control of the area, and East Bengal (now Bangladesh) became a separate kingdom called Samatata. After that, the Harsha Empire was in power.

Gopala was the first Buddhist king in Bangladesh. In 750, he founded the Pala dynasty, an empire that would

Early Empires, ca. 250 B.C.–A.D. 1700

Maximum extent of control

Mauryan Empire, ca. 250 B.C.

Sena dynasty, ca. A.D. 1200

Gupta dynasty, ca. A.D. 400

Delhi Sultanate, ca. A.D. 1300

Pala dynasty, ca. A.D. 800

Mughal Empire, ca. A.D. 1700

last for four centuries. During that time, Buddhism spread throughout the region. In 1150, the Senas took over, bringing the Hindu religion with them.

Times Begin to Change

In the early 1200s, Islam established a strong foothold in the region when Muslims from central Asia took control of Bengal. Their rule is called the Delhi Sultanate. They remained in power for hundreds of years until Akbar the Great, the Muslim ruler of the Mughal Empire, arrived. The Mughal Empire covered most of what is now India, Pakistan, and Afghanistan.

An Ancient Mound

Not far outside the town of Bogra on the bank of the Karatoa River is Mohasthangarh, the oldest archaeological site in Bangladesh. The site, which dates back to 2500 B.C., is sacred to Hindus even today. Every twelve years in December, thousands of worshippers travel to Mohasthangarh to join in a ritual bathing ceremony along the Karatoa.

Mohasthangarh rises out of the ground around it. It looks like a gigantic grass-covered mound. Its oblong shape measures roughly 5,000 feet (1,500 m) by 4,500 feet (1,400 m).

Mohasthangarh is one of the most popular tourist sites in Bangladesh. Visitors enjoy exploring its museum, where they can see the pots, gold ornaments, and coins that have been dug up in the area.

Akbar the Great ascended to the throne in his early teens and ruled for nearly fifty years.

Akbar took over most of Bengal by 1576, and people began converting to Islam. In 1608, Dhaka was founded and became the capital of the empire's Bengal Province.

Starting in the 1400s, European traders also came to South Asia. As the years went by and their numbers climbed, their influence was felt ever more strongly. In 1600, the East India Company was formed in Great Britain. Its mission was to develop trade with India and the Far East. Previously, Europeans had depended on Arab traders to bring them goods from these places. But many Europeans envied the success of the Arab traders and wanted to find their own route to South Asia.

The East India Company grew quickly. In time, it came to control almost all of what is now India, Pakistan, and Bangladesh. The company officially took control of the region after the Battle of Plassey in 1757. In this battle, the English were under the command of Robert Clive, an agent of the East India Company. They managed to defeat the local ruler's forces, largely through bribery and deception.

The East India Company immersed itself in the political and military matters of the region. The British leaders soon wanted the Bengalis and Indians to be more like them. They changed the schools so that classes were taught in

The British who worked for the East India Company prospered while the company controlled much of South Asia.

English, subtly passing on the lesson that being British was, in many ways, superior. The British also altered the region's strong textile industry. Previously, the people of South Asia had been exporting muslin and silk clothing to European countries. The British wanted the local people to use British machine-made fabric because it was cheaper. They flooded the local markets with the machine-made cloth. It wasn't long before the clothing quality declined and with it, the industry itself.

Although the East India Company was thriving, little of its success was filtering down to the people. The company did nothing to improve their lives. Finally, in 1857, the people began the Indian Rebellion, also known as the Sepoy Mutiny or the First War of Independence. The rebellion lasted for months, and many people were killed on both sides. In the end, the Indians gave in, but by then the East India Company was ready to let the British government take over in its place. The result was the birth of British India. This era is also known as the British Raj, from an ancient word for "king."

Under British Rule

India was the "jewel in the crown" of the British Empire. Bengal became one of the seventeen provinces of British

India. Under British rule, the western half of Bengal, which was primarily Hindu, saw economic improvements. Eastern Bengal, which was mostly Muslim, continued to struggle.

In 1905, the British divided Bengal into two provinces: East Bengal, with its capital of Dhaka, and West Bengal, with its capital of Calcutta. The Hindus of western Bengal did not like this decision because they feared that a divided province would leave them with less power. The Muslims in the east, however, favored the split. Soon, rioting began, and in 1911, the separation was reversed. By then, the dislike between the Hindu and Muslim populations ran deep and strong. It would continue in the coming decades.

By the 1940s, the people of British India were demanding independence. Finally, in 1947, Britain granted India its independence. But the hostility between Hindus and Muslims convinced the British to divide India along religious lines. Most Muslims lived in the northwest and the east. These regions became the new nation of Pakistan.

Bengal was divided between the two newly independent countries. Hindu West Bengal became part of India. Muslim East Bengal became

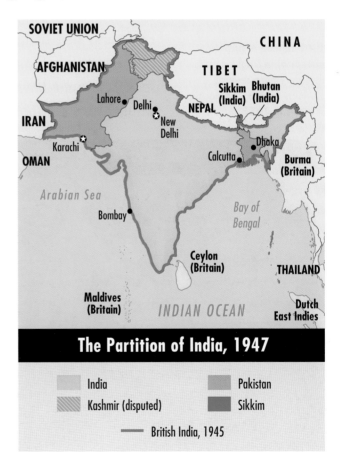

The Partition of India, 1947

India
Kashmir (disputed)
Pakistan
Sikkim
British India, 1945

part of Pakistan. In time, it would become known as East Pakistan. The other part would be called West Pakistan. The two halves of Pakistan did not even touch. In fact, 1,000 miles (1,600 km) of Indian territory lay between the two.

The Pakistani Years

Pakistan's government, businesses, and armed forces were based in West Pakistan, so most of the country's money and power were there. But East Pakistan had most of the people, and they were hungry and poor. East Pakistanis and West Pakistanis had little in common. Though both groups were Muslim, they had different cultures and traditions. They even spoke different languages. It was the issue of language that would prove the most troublesome.

The Shaheed Minar memorial in Dhaka marks the site where several students were killed during protests in 1952.

Leaders and scholars in West Pakistan wanted Urdu to be the nation's official language, even though fewer than 7 percent of the people living in East and West Pakistan could speak it. The people in the east wanted Bangla, which is often called Bengali, to be the official language, since that is what most Pakistanis spoke. After West Pakistan declared Urdu the new national language, riots broke out. The police shot and killed several students at a demonstration in Dhaka on February 21, 1952. It was clear that this issue was vitally important to the people. At last, the government agreed to declare Urdu and Bangla equal official languages.

February 21 is now called Martyr's Day or Language Movement Day to honor those who died standing up for their beliefs. A memorial was built at the site where the students were killed. Each year, hundreds of thousands of people bring flowers to the memorial to honor those who died.

The Bhola Cyclone of 1970 killed hundreds of thousands of people, destroyed countless homes, and devastated crops.

Civil War

In 1970, everything began to change for East Pakistan. First, a horrific cyclone and tidal wave struck, killing more than half a million people. The government was slow to respond to the chaos. The people of East Pakistan were desperate and frustrated by their government's lack of leadership and aid.

In December, elections were held. The Awami League, a Muslim political party based in East Pakistan, secured a solid majority of seats in the National Assembly. The party was led by Sheikh Mujibur Rahman, who was generally called Sheikh Mujib. Mujib had built his platform on the idea of self-government

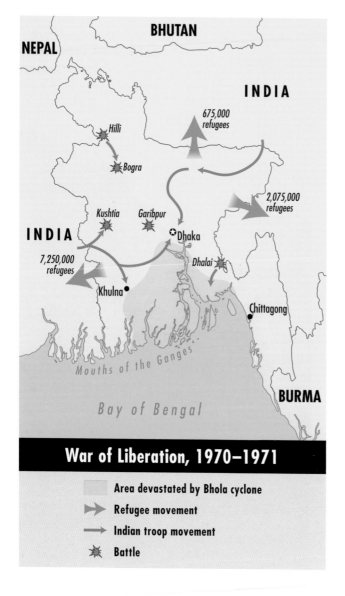

War of Liberation, 1970–1971

- Area devastated by Bhola cyclone
- Refugee movement
- Indian troop movement
- Battle

Map labels: NEPAL, BHUTAN, INDIA, Hilli, Bogra, 675,000 refugees, 2,075,000 refugees, Kushtia, Garibpur, Dhaka, INDIA, 7,250,000 refugees, Dhalai, Khulna, Chittagong, Mouths of the Ganges, Bay of Bengal, BURMA

for East Pakistan. He wanted it to become an independent nation called Bangladesh.

A few months after the elections, President Yahya Kan, the same leader who had done little to help victims of the cyclone, refused to let the new National Assembly meet. This prevented Mujib from becoming its leader. East Pakistanis protested, and their frustration grew. West Pakistan sent armed forces into East Pakistan and arrested Mujib. Civil war broke out, and on March 26, 1971, the East Pakistanis declared their independence. More than ten million people fled to India to escape the fighting.

West Pakistan had expelled all foreign journalists before arresting Mujib, so the rest of the world knew little about what was going on. After almost nine months of intense fighting, Indira Gandhi, the prime minister of India, stepped in to help by sending India's army to support the East Pakistanis. West Pakistan admitted defeat in December 1971. More than a million people had given their lives in the fight for Bangladesh's independence.

Home at Last

It took thirty-five years, but in 2006, the Bangladeshi people were at last able to give one of their heroes the tribute they felt he so richly deserved.

It all began in August 1971, four months before Bangladesh won its independence from Pakistan. Matiur Rahman, a flight lieutenant in the Pakistan Air Force, was trying something unbelievably daring and dangerous.

On the morning of August 20, he climbed into a T-33 training jet. He was supposedly there to train a student to fly the plane. But his real plan was to take control of the aircraft midflight and get it to Bengali forces fighting for independence. The plan was a good one, but doomed. The plane crashed in Thatta, near the Indian border. Rahman's body was found near the crash site, and he was quickly buried in a graveyard at the airbase reserved for fourth-class employees. The Pakistani government declared him a traitor. The Bengalis hailed him as a hero.

Thirty-five years later, Bangladeshi prime minister Khaleda Zia made a formal request to have Rahman's remains returned to his homeland. Pakistan agreed. In April 2006, the daring young lieutenant's remains were given to Bangladesh. Thousands of people came to pay their respects to Rahman as he was buried. The Bangladeshi military awarded Rahman the *Bir Sreshtho*, its highest honor. In addition, the Bangladesh Air Force Base in Jessore was renamed the Matiur Rahman Air Base.

The Young Nation

Mujibur Rahman was released from prison in January 1972 and returned to Bangladesh to serve as its prime minister. Unfortunately, he was not nearly as skilled at leading people as he was at inspiring them. He chose people for important political positions based on their loyalty to him, rather than on their abilities. He also made poor economic decisions.

When a severe flood hit the country in 1974, killing thousands of people and destroying crops, Bangladeshis' suffering

Sheikh Mujibur Rahman (center) was pivotal in helping Bangladesh gain independence, though he proved to be a poor leader.

increased once again. Millions were left homeless, food supplies were severely limited, and hospitals, factories, and schools were ruined. A cholera epidemic swept through the country, killing many people, while starvation killed even more.

But still the government did little. In 1975, Sheikh Mujib took the position of president and declared Bangladesh a one-party state. By the end of the year, this once-heroic man was assassinated in a military coup.

For two years, the military ruled Bangladesh. At the end of 1976, army general Zia-ur Rahman declared himself in charge and named himself president. The people officially elected him in 1978, and in 1979, he was made head of the Bangladesh National Party. Then, in 1981, he too was assassinated.

Vice President Abdus Sattar became president, but only for a brief time. In 1982, he was overthrown in a coup led by Hussain Muhammad Ershad, the former chief of staff of the Bangladeshi army. Ershad immediately suspended the country's constitution and banned other political parties. He established martial law, putting the military in control of the country.

In 1986, Ershad resigned from the army so that he could run as a civilian in the presidential election. After he was elected, he ended martial law and put the constitution into effect again. Despite his apparent success, many people did not like or trust him. Most felt that the elections had been dishonest. In 1987, a state of emergency was called in response to repeated strikes and demonstrations against him. When 1988 brought severe flooding, people got angrier as their government did not provide the help they so desperately needed.

Finally, in late 1990, Ershad was forced to resign. When rumors began to fly that he was about to be arrested, he tried to flee but was caught. The following year, people's suspicions were proven correct—he was tried and convicted of several counts of corruption and of the illegal possession of arms.

After Ershad was forced out of office, Begum Khaleda Zia, the widow of President Zia-ur Rahman, became prime minister. At the time, the constitution was changed so that the position of president would be mostly ceremonial. Instead, the prime minister would have the power.

Khaleda Zia, the first woman prime minister of Bangladesh, was first elected in 1991. After a term out of office, she was elected again in 2001.

In 1996, the Awami League won the elections. Sheikh Hasina Wajed, the daughter of Mujibur Rahman, became prime minister. Five years later, Khaleda Zia returned to power. Though power has passed smoothly from one prime minister to the next, elections continue to be marred by accusations of fraud and outbreaks of violence. Bangladesh is still a young nation, and it has not yet reached a point where it has a stable government.

Seeking
Stability

BANGLADESH FOUGHT HARD TO ACHIEVE ITS INDEPEN-
dence. Some of the battle involved finding honest, wise, and
reliable leadership. Too many times, Bangladeshi leaders have
turned out to be not at all what the people had hoped for. This
has led to decades of political instability.

Opposite: **People gather at a protest against religious militancy.**

Running the Country

The government of Bangladesh has three branches: executive,
legislative, and judicial.

The executive branch is responsible for making the rules
for the government. It is officially headed by the president, but
the president has little actual power. The person who truly leads
the country is the prime minister. Both offices have five-year
terms. The president is elected by the parliament. The prime
minister is chosen from the political party that wins the most
seats in the parliament. The prime minister appoints cabinet

The National Flag of Bangladesh

Bangladesh's flag is green with a red circle in
the middle. The green background represents
the nation's vital, fertile ground, while the red
circle stands for the rising sun and the sacrifice
people made for their country's independence.
The flag was adopted on January 13, 1972.

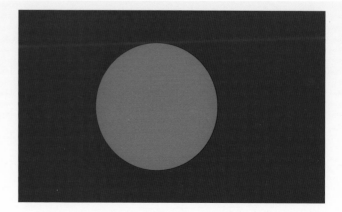

Parliament meets in the National Assembly building in Dhaka.

NATIONAL GOVERNMENT OF BANGLADESH

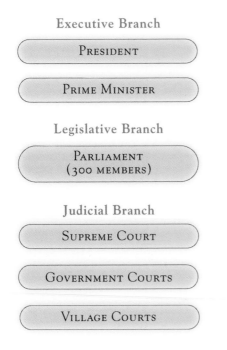

Executive Branch

(PRESIDENT)

(PRIME MINISTER)

Legislative Branch

(PARLIAMENT (300 MEMBERS))

Judicial Branch

(SUPREME COURT)

(GOVERNMENT COURTS)

(VILLAGE COURTS)

members to head various departments. In 2006, the president of Bangladesh was Iajuddin Ahmed, and the prime minister was Khaleda Zia.

Bangladesh's legislative branch consists of a one-house parliament called the *Jatiya Sangsad*, or "House of the People." The parliament has three hundred members who are elected by the people for five-year terms. The parliament meets in the National Assembly building, perhaps the most renowned building in Bangladesh. This simple but powerful building was designed by American architect Louis Kahn.

The judicial branch is made up of the nation's courts. The highest court in Bangladesh is the Supreme Court. The president appoints the Supreme Court justices, who oversee the lower courts, including government and village courts.

Taking Part

Over the years, the number of political parties in Bangladesh has grown. The largest are the Awami League, the Bangladesh Nationalist Party, and the Jatiya Party. Bangladeshis must be eighteen to vote.

Bangladesh established its own military in 1972. It is made up of volunteers who are at least seventeen years old. The army has about one hundred thousand members, while the navy has nine thousand, and the air force has six thousand.

Bangladesh soldiers march in a parade in Dhaka. Service in the Bangladesh military is voluntary.

Violence Breeds Violence

Although Bangladesh has made a great deal of progress, its government is still not stable or trustworthy. Past leaders have been convicted of crimes, and political violence remains a constant threat.

Bombs frequently disrupt life in Bangladesh. In April 2001, seven people were killed in bomb blasts at a New Year's concert in Dhaka. In June, a bomb placed in a Roman Catholic church in Baniarchar exploded, killing ten people. Two months later, eight people were killed and hundreds injured as two bombs went off at an election rally in southwestern Bangladesh.

Protests in Bangladesh sometimes turn violent.

Political activists gather at a rally in Dhaka.

And the violence continues. In 2004, a grenade attack in Dhaka killed twenty-two. In January 2005, Awami League politician Shah A. M. S. Kibria was killed by a grenade at a political rally. Eight months later, 350 small bombs exploded in towns and cities across the nation, and two people were killed. Events like these can only damage the progress the government has made.

As Professor Nanda R. Shrestha, who studies South Asia, writes: "If the current regime continues to walk down the path of physical violence and revenge against its opposition parties, as it seems to have done so far, it will have only succeeded in perpetuating the cycle of violence and in undermining national interests. Such a path will only make a mockery of democracy. . . . After all, in politics, what goes around, comes around. Violence breeds more violence."

Bangladesh's National Anthem

One of Bangladesh's most prolific and beloved poets, Rabindranath Tagore, wrote the words and music to the national anthem, "Amar Shonar Bangia," or "My Golden Bengal."

My Bengal of gold, I love you
Forever your skies, your air set my
heart in tune as if it were a flute,
In Spring, Oh mother mine, the
fragrance from your mango-groves
makes me wild with joy—
Ah, what a thrill!
In Autumn, Oh mother mine,
in the full-blossomed paddy fields,
I have seen spread all over—sweet smiles!
Ah, what a beauty, what shades,
what an affection
and what a tenderness!
What a quilt have you spread at the feet
of banyan trees and along the banks of rivers!
Oh mother mine, words from your
lips are like Nectar to my ears!
Ah, what a thrill!
If sadness, Oh mother mine, casts a gloom
on your face, my eyes are filled with tears!

Dhaka: Did You Know This?

The capital city of Dhaka was founded in 1608. It served as a Mughal provincial capital until 1704 and then became one of the area's busiest trading centers for the French, English, and Dutch.

Dhaka is located in almost the exact center of the nation. It is the largest city in Bangladesh, spreading over about 315 square miles (816 sq km). Almost nineteen million people squeeze into that area. The streets of Dhaka are jammed full of people. Cars and other vehicles sit in bumper-to-bumper traffic. And winding in between the people and the cars are colorful rickshaws.

The bustling city is Bangladesh's industrial, commercial, cultural, and political center. With temperatures that rarely rise above 90°F (32°C) in the summer or dip below 50°F (10°C) in the winter, Dhaka is the perfect place to spend some time.

Dhaka is a delightful blend of the old and the new. The city is filled with mosques dating back to the seventeenth and eighteenth centuries. The Lalbagh Fort was built in 1648. It was the scene of a vicious battle in 1971 during Bangladesh's fight for independence. Open-air markets are scattered throughout the city. Items do not have a set price. Instead, shoppers haggle and bargain. For people who prefer a more modern place to shop, the city also features the largest mall in South Asia.

The National Martyr's Monument is one of the most famous sites in Dhaka. It is dedicated to the memory of the more than one million people who died in the War of Liberation. Dhaka's museums include the National Art Gallery and the Bangabandhu Memorial Museum, the former home of Mujibur Rahman. Dhaka is also the site of the Banga Bhaban, the official residence of the nation's president.

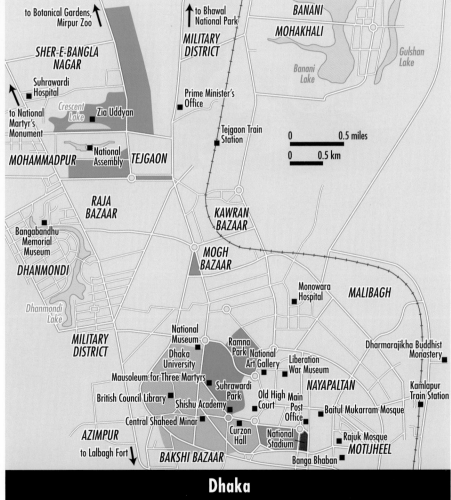

Dhaka

The Struggle to Survive

64

Workers unload sand from a ship in Dhaka. Sand is used to make cement, one of the few products that is manufactured in Bangladesh.

BANGLADESH HAS MANY THINGS TO BE PROUD OF. IT HAS beautiful waterways and majestic animals, and it has achieved a hard-fought independence. But its people continue to struggle from day to day for the basic necessities of life. Bangladesh is one of the poorest nations on the planet.

About 45 percent of Bangladeshis live below the poverty line, spending their lives working hard for little money. Unemployment is extremely high and jobs are prized, even if they are physically demanding and pay little. Many young people move to countries such as Saudi Arabia, Singapore, Kuwait, and Malaysia to find work.

Opposite: **Rice is kept in rows as it dries at a processing plant in Dhaka.**

The Struggle to Survive **65**

With a Little Help from Their Friends

In 1971, Bangladesh was struggling to gain independence and recover from yet another devastating flood. Indian musician Ravi Shankar had an idea: he would call an English friend for help. His friend was George Harrison, who had been part of the Beatles, one of the most popular rock bands in history. Harrison said he would be happy to help—and he did so in an amazing way. In a mere five weeks, he organized a huge concert at New York City's Madison Square Garden. As he phrased it in a song during the concert:

My friend came to me,
With sadness in his eyes,
He told me that he wanted help,
Before his country died,

Although I couldn't feel the pain,
I knew I'd have to try,
Now I'm asking all of you,
To help us save some lives.

On August 1, 1971, more than forty thousand people came to hear rock legends like Harrison, Ringo Starr, Eric Clapton, and Bob Dylan play. The album recorded during that concert stayed at the top of the charts for forty-one weeks. The concert raised $250,000, and later album and movie sales added millions more. Since then, many other musicians have followed the lead of Ravi Shankar and George Harrison, using concerts to raise money and bring attention to causes they believe in.

Working the Land

Most Bangladeshis work in agriculture. The rich soil of Bangladesh produces abundant rice, a staple of the Bangladeshi diet. Much of the country's flat land is used for rice fields. Seeds are planted in the rainy season and grow underwater. Later, the rice is harvested by hand. This is the old-fashioned, least expensive way to grow rice. Sometimes, farmers use oxen to pull a plow and a stick to dig holes for each seed. The patches of land are often so small that there is not enough room for modern mechanical farm equipment.

Most farmers in Bangladesh still use traditional farming methods, such as plowing with oxen.

Bangladesh also produces enormous amounts of jute, a plant used for making rope, baskets, fishing nets, and carpet backing. Bangladesh is the largest producer of the fiber in the world. More than 75 percent of the country's export money comes from jute.

Jute grows underwater in long, slender shoots about the width of a finger. Each shoot can reach as tall as 15 feet (4.5 m), and all of its leaves are on the top half of the stalk. Harvesting jute requires a huge amount of labor. Workers first tie bundles of stalks together and then leave them until all of the leaves fall off. Next, the stalks are soaked for a month

It takes more than a month from the time a jute plant is cut until its fiber can be spun into usable thread.

An Experiment in Banking

In 1976, Muhammad Yunus, a professor of rural economics at the University of Chittagong, had had it. He was tired of seeing the poor get poorer in Bangladesh. He had an idea for a new research project. He wanted to see what would happen if he created a banking system that provided credit to the poor. In the banking world, that was a radical idea.

His idea turned into the Grameen Bank Project. (*Grameen* is Bangla for "rural" or "village".) The plan was simple: extend banking services to the poor; create opportunities for the poor to be self-employed; and reverse the vicious circle of "low income, low saving, and low investment" into the much more positive "low income, more savings, more investment, more income" circle. With this system, Yunus believed that he could eliminate poverty. "One day," he once said, "our grandchildren will go to museums to see what poverty was like."

More than 95 percent of the people who borrow money from the Grameen Bank are female. That is because there is a long history in Bangladesh of men spending their family's money on drinking or gambling. Men who want to borrow money from the Grameen Bank face a much more complicated application process.

Though the Grameen Bank has not eliminated poverty, it has been a great success. The loans are small, and an amazing 98 percent of them are repaid in full. These loans have enabled many women to start their own small businesses. Borrowing is easy; interest is fair.

"Poverty covers people in a thick crust and makes the poor appear stupid and without initiative," says Yunus. "Yet if you give them credit, they will slowly come back to life." He adds, "People say I am crazy, but no one can achieve anything without a dream. . . . If one is going to make headway against poverty, one cannot do business as usual. One must be revolutionary and think the unthinkable." In 2006, Yunus was awarded the Nobel Peace Prize for his revolutionary idea of giving loans to the poor.

until they soften. The fiber is stripped from the plants by workers standing in water up to their waists.

The fibers are washed and draped over poles to dry in the sun. When they are completely dry, they are tied in bundles and put on boats to be taken to mills. There, they will be spun into threads and turned into a variety of products. Jute mills are located in Jessore, Chandpur, and Chittagong.

Tea is another major crop in Bangladesh. It is grown primarily in the Sylhet Hills of the northeast. More than one hundred thousand people work harvesting tea between the months of March and December. While a great deal of the tea is shipped to Europe, even more of it stays in the country for Bangladeshis to drink.

Wheat is grown in the southern part of the country. It is used to make a flatbread called chappati. Other crops grown in Bangladesh include sugarcane, potatoes, spices, legumes, and fruit. While some of these products are exported, most go to feed the millions of hungry Bangladeshis.

Map

NEPAL

INDIA

INDIA

Goats

Wheat

Tobacco

Cattle

Rajshahi

Wheat

Dhaka

Narayanganj

Potatoes

Sugarcane

Khulna

Salt

Salt Salt

Chittagong

Tea

Mouths of the Ganges

Bay of Bengal

MYANMAR (BURMA)

Resources

Cereals (mainly rice)	**C** Coal	**NG** Natural gas
Forest	**Cem** Cement	**Salt** Salt
	Fe Iron	**Ti** Titanium
Pasture livestock	**Fz** Fertilizer	**Oil** Oil

Women harvest tea in
the hills of northeastern
Bangladesh.

What Bangladesh Grows, Makes, and Mines

Agriculture

Rice (2000)	35,820,000 metric tons
Wheat (2000)	6,950,000 metric tons
Jute (2001)	1,530,000 metric tons

Manufacturing

Cement (2001)	2,340,000 metric tons
Fertilizer (2001)	1,875,000 metric tons
Jute goods (2002)	536,000 metric tons

Mining (2002)

Natural gas	11,200,000,000 cubic meters
Limestone	32,000 metric tons
Kaolin	8,100 metric tons

Few people in Bangladesh own the land that they farm. Instead, they live on someone else's land, tending and harvesting the crops. They sell the crops and turn over most of the profit to the landowner. This system is called sharecropping. While it benefits the landowners, the people doing the hard work make barely enough money to put food on the table. Most farmers plant two or three crops each year, if possible, to make the most of the land they have.

Fishing and Livestock

With its abundant water, many Bangladeshis make a living catching fish. Fishermen, or *majhi*, spend hours on the water each day to catch enough fish for their families to eat along with some extras to sell at a market. They typically use hand-held nets to bring in their catches. Some Bangladeshis have shrimp and frog farms. These creatures are eaten locally or exported to India, Japan, North America, the Middle East, and Europe.

Livestock also play a role in Bangladesh's economy. Cattle are used for plowing and transporting crops. They are also eaten, and their hides are used as leather. At least half the people in Bangladesh own some kind of livestock. Men typically take care of cattle and buffalo, while women and children tend poultry, goats, and sheep.

Majhi use nets to catch shrimp larvae to supply shrimp farms.

Few Bangladeshi workers are involved in industry. The country's major factory products include paper, steel, cement, fertilizer, clothing, and jute products. Many items exported from Bangladesh are made by hand. These include embroidered cloth, leather goods, and terra-cotta pottery. Bangladesh is rich in natural gas, but most of it is used by Bangladeshis. Little remains for export.

Workers spin jute fibers into thread.

Breaking a Ship

In Bangladesh, one way to make money is to break a ship apart. This has been a source of income for Bangladeshis for almost forty years. Breaking ships provides desperate Banlgadeshis with much-needed money and recycles countless materials, but it is dangerous work.

Even the biggest and best ships are eventually retired. Whether they are deluxe ocean liners or durable freighters, many of them are brought to the port of Chittagong to be taken apart, piece by piece. A number of companies bid on the retired ships, and the highest bid wins. It can cost more than three million dollars to buy one of these old ships, but by the time it has been stripped and the materials resold and recycled, the buyer has made a profit.

Taking apart a ship begins after the ship's captain does the one thing that captains are taught never to do: steer the boat up onto the beach. Once it is secure, Bangladeshi workers, including young children, scramble across it. Some carry welding torches to cut out pieces of steel. Others carry sledgehammers for breaking up walls and removing equipment. Everything from doorknobs and toilets to drops of oil that remain in the tanks is removed, to be sold or reused. Much of the scrap metal is melted down and sold. It takes about eight weeks to entirely break apart a large ship.

Some groups want to ban ship breaking because it is risky for the workers. There are no safety standards. No one wears hard hats or safety boots. No one wears a harness when working high up. At least one person dies every day from this hazardous work. Some workers die from breathing toxic chemicals. Others are killed in explosions when torches ignite leftover fuel.

Bangladeshis take the risk in stride. In a country where it is often hard to find enough food to eat, they are willing to take on dangerous work for a meager paycheck. For now, breaking a ship is just another way to feed the family.

One of the country's biggest and steadiest businesses is the garment industry. When Bangladesh began exporting clothing in 1979, the industry made about $1 million a year. By 1986, that figure was up to $450 million. In 1997, the number was closer to $3.5 billion.

More than 1.5 million people, primarily young women between the ages of fourteen and twenty-nine, work in the garment business. It is tiring work. Most days last between fourteen and sixteen hours, and some workers bring home as

Some garment factories exploit young laborers.

little as fifteen dollars a month. Now and then, the workers have banded together to protest their low wages. Sometimes this makes a difference. Some garment shops now offer benefits and clean surroundings, while others are dangerously dirty and take advantage of young workers. The recently formed Bangladesh National Garment Workers Federation is trying to secure better conditions and wages for its members.

Handmade, Homemade

Many Bangladeshi products are crafts that date back hundreds of years. The leather-finishing industry, which uses the hides of cattle and goats, has been slowly growing. Unfortunately, many of the tanneries where the leatherwork is done emit huge amounts of toxic chemicals such as chromium. Frequent exposure to chromium can damage the liver, kidneys, immune system, and nervous system, as well as increase a person's overall cancer risk.

Weights and Measures

Bangladesh uses the metric system of weights and measures. In this system, the basic unit of weight is the kilogram, which equals 2.2 pounds. The basic unit of length is the meter, which equals 39.37 inches.

Bangladeshis have a long tradition of making decorated terra-cotta pots. People use the pots to carry liquids or store food. Every Bangladeshi kitchen has a few. Bangladeshis also make special pieces like the *shokher hari*, a pot used for weddings, and the *shora*, a lid to put on top of cooking pots.

Handmade terra-cotta pots are a staple in Bangladeshi homes.

Other Bangladeshi traditions include weaving straw and bamboo. Straw mats are used on a daily basis in Bangladesh. People sit on them, sleep on them, and use them to cover their floors. Many women use colored straw to weave patterns and designs in their mats. *Botni* mats are made for husbands and fathers to take to prayer. A *sitalpati*, or cool mat, is made from sugarcane that is first soaked in water and then woven.

Some women make ornate embroidered quilts called *nakshi kantha*. The quilts usually feature traditional designs such as water lilies, tigers, or the sun and stars. They often tell a story of some kind and are considered works of art.

Traditional carpets and mats are woven from many different materials, including golden jute fibers.

Colorful Money

The currency used in Bangladesh is called *taka*. Each taka is divided into 100 *poisha*. Bills come in denominations of 1, 2, 5, 10, 20, 50, 100, and 500 takas. Coins come in denominations of 1, 5, 10, 25, and 50 poishas. There are also 1- and 5-taka coins. In 2006, 1 taka was worth US$0.01439, and US$1 was worth 69.45 taka.

The colors and symbols on taka are delicate and meaningful. The images reflect both daily life and the nation's history and fight for independence. The 2-taka note, for example, carries pictures of both the Language Martyrs' Monument and the doel, which is the national bird. Other bills have images of the Bagha Mosque of Rajshahi, the National Martyr's Monument in Dhaka, a hand holding up rice plants, and the country's famous spotted deer.

Hope for the Future

Although the economic situation in Bangladesh has long been dire, some progress is being made. Exports continue to grow, and some businesses are thriving. Thanks to systems like the Grameen Bank Project, which lends money to the poor, things are slowly improving. Given enough time, perhaps foreigners will think of Bangladesh as a country of beautiful waterways rather than a crowded nation filled with hungry people.

Life and Language

BANGLADESHIS MAY BE POOR, BUT THEY ARE FULL OF pride, determination, and faith. Their food is often meager, but it is shared with any visitor who comes by. Bangladeshis are also eager to share a story and a cup of hot, sweet tea.

Most Bangladeshis live in rural villages on incredibly small pieces of land. Their homes are simple, with only one or two rooms, and they rarely have electricity or plumbing. The walls are made of bamboo and the roofs are thatched. Often, these homes are clustered together with a common courtyard in the middle where people gather.

Opposite: **Almost one-third of the Bangladeshi population is under fifteen.**

Children study and a woman cooks outside of their village home.

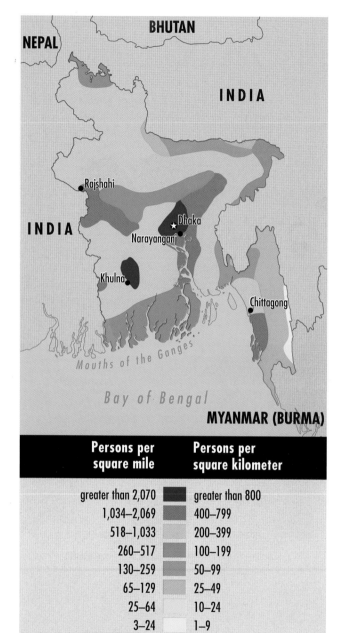

Persons per square mile		Persons per square kilometer
greater than 2,070		greater than 800
1,034–2,069		400–799
518–1,033		200–399
260–517		100–199
130–259		50–99
65–129		25–49
25–64		10–24
3–24		1–9

Living in the city is too expensive for most Bangladeshis. Those who do manage it are found in *bustees*, or large slums. Their homes are made out of scraps of wood or sheets of tin, plastic, or cardboard. Only the wealthiest live in homes made out of brick or concrete.

Family Life

Families tend to be large, with at least four children. There are several reasons for this. Families want as many children as possible to help in the fields or with other work. Also, some parents want to have many children so that there will always be someone to take care of them when they get old.

Most households center around the *poribar*, the extended family. It includes parents and their single children as well as married sons and their families. The eldest male is the head of the family and makes most of the decisions. Women spend their days looking after animals, preparing food, watching over children, and talking to one another.

Men and women in Bangladesh are not treated equally. It is unusual for a woman to leave her village. Women are confined in many places, although this is slowly beginning to change. Girls are taught from an early age to obey their fathers and husbands. Many women will never own their own business or property.

A woman cooks over a small clay stove.

Mind Your Manners

Bangladeshi society has many rules of behavior that must be followed. For example, people entering a home, temple, or mosque must remove their shoes, yet they should not expose the soles of their feet. Blowing your nose at the dinner table is the height of bad manners, but burping is considered completely normal. Respect for elders is required. Elders are allowed to eat and speak first at all times. Looking directly into an older person's eyes or disagreeing with someone older is avoided.

Most Bangladeshis are Muslim, and traditional Muslim practice divides men and women even further. If the family follows the Islamic rule of *purdah*, for example, boys and girls are separated after they reach puberty. They sit and sleep in

Boys study the Qur'an at a madrassa, an Islamic school.

Writer Taslima Nasrin has lived in exile in Europe since the mid-1990s.

different places in the home, sit in different areas if they go to school, and are not allowed to shake hands with or look directly at each other in public. Single people are never supposed to make public displays of affection. Even married couples are not supposed to kiss or hug in public, as that is considered immoral and disgraceful.

How strong is the belief in Bangladesh that men and women are unequal? When author Taslima Nasrin wrote a series of articles in which she criticized the way women are treated, some people called for her death. Her books are now banned in Bangladesh, and she is forced to live outside the country.

Major Cities in Bangladesh (2003)

Dhaka	18.7 million
Chittagong	5 million
Khulna	2.4 million

Most girls and boys are taught in separate classrooms.

Life in and out of School

The average life span of a Bangladeshi is quite short when compared with the rest of the world. Most people do not live past sixty, and only 3.5 percent of the nation's population is over sixty-five years old.

About 33 percent of Bangladeshis are under fourteen. Few of these children are in school. Though Bangladeshi law requires that young children go to elementary school for five years, at least half of them stay home to help their families. School is too expensive for many. There are some *madrassas*, or Islamic schools, that offer free education to the poor. They provide food, shelter, and a full education in the ways of Islam.

Because so few Bangladeshis go to school, the country has a low literacy rate. Just 43 percent of adults can read and write. Traditionally, girls were much less likely to be educated than boys. As a result, only 32 percent of women can read and write, while 54 percent of men can. This will probably change in the future, however, because girls and boys are now equally likely to go to school. Bangladesh has several universities, including Rajshahi University, Chittagong University, and the University of Dhaka.

The University of Dhaka opened in 1921.

Talking Bangla

Asalaam alaykum	Hello (to a Muslim)
Nomaashkaar	Hello (to a Hindu)
Khudaa hafiz	Good-bye
Pore dakhaa hobe	See you later
Maaf korun	Excuse me
Ji	Yes
Naa	No
Tik aache	No problem
Kaamon aachen?	How are you?
Bhaalo aahi	I'm fine
Aapnaar naam ki?	What's your name?
Aami bujhi naa	I don't understand
Aami jaabo . . .	I want to go to . . .
Kotaai . . . ?	Where is . . . ?
Koto dur . . . ?	How far is . . . ?

The Importance of Language

In a country where education is limited, it is interesting to note how important language is. It is so important, in fact, that people gave up their lives for it during the Pakistani years. To the people of Bangladesh, language is an indication of pride in their country. They love listening to stories and poetry.

While English is spoken in the cities, almost everywhere else people speak Bangla, a mixture of Portuguese, Farsi, Arabic, and Hindi. Two different types of Bangla are spoken. *Sadhubhasa* is an elegant language that dates to the sixteenth century. It is rarely used by the common people. Instead, they use *chaltibhasa*, the casual, twentieth-century language that is taught in school.

A sign on a beach at Cox's Bazaar is in Bangla and English.

More than ten newspapers are published in Dhaka. Most are in Bangla, some are in English, and others are in both.

Bangla is written in a wavy script that is similar to the script used for some other languages in South Asia. The Bangla script uses no capital or lowercase letters. Instead, all letters have only one case.

A Dozen Different Tribes

About 98 percent of the people in Bangladesh are Bengali. The country's only minorities are the tribal communities in the Chittagong Hills of the southeast. Unlike the rest of the population, they speak languages other than Bangla and are neither Muslim nor Hindu, but Buddhist.

The tribal groups include the Chakma, Marma, Mro, Tripura, Tengchangya, Khumi, Lushai, Panku, Sak, Bown, Kuki, and Reang. Collectively, they are known as the Jumma

The Chakma are known for their beautiful traditional weavings.

and number just over one million. The Chakma are the largest group, making up about half the entire tribal population. The Marma and the Tripura are the next largest. The rest of the tribes are quite small.

Tribal groups speak their own languages. They also have their own lifestyles, rites, customs, and food. It is often easy to tell them from the Bengalis. Their skin is a lighter shade of brown, and they commonly wear handwoven garments. Some women wear long, thick necklaces that look like glittering bibs. The Jumma are constantly on the move, never settling in one place for too long. Like the Bengalis, however, the Jumma are all quite poor. Most depend on farming to make a living. They use a slash-and-burn technique of cutting down plants, burning what is left, and then replanting in the burned area.

The Jumma and the Bengalis are often at odds with each other. In the 1960s, when a dam was built in the Chittagong Hills, a huge swath of Jumma land was flooded. Thousands of people were forced from their homes. Tensions have also arisen because over the years the government has tried to convert the Jumma to Islam. In the process, more than four hundred thousand Bengalis have moved to the Chittagong Hill Tracts. People have been killed as the two groups battle over who has rights to the land.

Ethnic Bangladesh

Bengalis	98%
Non-Bengali Muslims and tribal groups	2%

A Tripura woman forages for firewood.

The Paths to God

Rᴇʟɪɢɪᴏɴ ɪs ᴀ ᴠɪᴛᴀʟ ᴘᴀʀᴛ ᴏғ ʟɪғᴇ ɪɴ Bᴀɴɢʟᴀᴅᴇsʜ. The vast majority of people are Muslims. It was not always that way, however. Long ago, Hinduism was the main religion throughout eastern Bengal. By the late 1800s, most of the population had converted to Islam, and a century later, in 1988, Islam was declared the official religion of Bangladesh. Today, only about 17 percent of Bangladeshis follow other religions, mainly Hinduism. Buddhism, Christianity, and animism are also practiced.

Opposite: **Some of the most striking buildings in Bangladesh are centers of worship, such as this mosque near Sonargaon.**

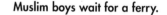

Muslim boys wait for a ferry.

Major Religions of Bangladesh

Islam	83 percent
Hinduism	16 percent
Other	1 percent

The Pillars of Islam

People who follow Islam are called Muslims. Islam began in the 600s in what is now Saudi Arabia when the Prophet Muhammad is said to have received messages from God. These messages were collected into the Qur'an. Early in its history, the religion divided into two factions, the Sunni and the Shi'i. Most Bangladeshi Muslims are Sunni.

Muslim men enter a mosque in Dhaka. Traditionally, only men prayed in mosques.

Islam is evident throughout the country. Mosques are everywhere. Five times a day (dawn, noon, midafternoon, sunset, and night), a person called a *muezzin* calls Muslims to prayer. The call is broadcast over loudspeakers in the largest cities.

Before entering a mosque, men wash their hands, feet, arms, and faces. To pray, they kneel on the ground facing Mecca, the holy city in Saudi Arabia where Islam began. They bend over until their heads touch the floor. In Bangladesh, women are traditionally not allowed in mosques.

Bangladeshi Muslims gather for afternoon prayers.

Major Muslim Holy Days

Islamic New Year
This is celebrated quietly with religious readings at home.

Moulid al-Nabi/Muhammad's Birthday
This day is spent thinking about how important Muhammad is to Muslims.

Ramadan
During this month, Muslims fast from sunrise to sundown.

Eid al-Fitr
This is the celebration of the end of Ramadan.

Eid al-Adha/Feast of Sacrifice
This feast honoring Abraham's obedience to God usually involves killing a lamb and sharing the meat with others.

Muslim children celebrate Eid al-Fitr.

Muslims are expected to carry out five basic duties, known as the Five Pillars of Islam. The first pillar, *shahada*, says that Muslims must make a declaration of faith. They do this by saying, "There is no god except God, and Muhammad is his prophet." The second pillar, *salat*, requires that Muslims pray five times a day. *Zakat*, the third pillar, says that Muslims must give help to those in need. The fourth pillar, *sawm*, requires that Muslims fast from sunrise to sunset during the month of Ramadan. This is to help them learn self-discipline and

A Self-Made Philosopher

Aroj Ali Matubbar (1900–1985) was a man of deep conviction. A devout Muslim, Matubbar made it his life mission to speak out to the world against religious fanaticism. He wanted to find a balance between science and religion.

Matubbar was a self-educated man. Because his father died when he was young, Matubbar had to work hard to support his family. Like many Bengali children, he was not able to go to school. Instead, he learned about the world by borrowing books from the library and friends. Over the years, he spent all of his spare money on books, and eventually he had his own personal library of several thousand volumes. Unfortunately, they were all lost in the 1961 cyclone.

Matubbar became friends with scholars who helped him publish his writings. His most famous books include *The Quest for Truth* and *The Mystery of Creation*. Matubbar once said, "I hate doing things which I don't understand by following others. To search for the truth is the passion of my life, serving humanity is my mission. I hate blind belief and superstition. . . . I don't wish to slumber in a boat anchored on the shore. I wish to travel wide awake in a speeding boat. I praise innovations, decry stagnation."

sympathy for the poor. And the final pillar, *hajj*, says that all Muslims should make a pilgrimage to Mecca once in their life if they are able to.

Muslims also follow many other rules about how to live. The Qur'an teaches about the importance of family and that people should be modest in their dress. Marriages are often arranged by parents, and men are allowed up to a total of four wives if they can treat them equally. In Bangladesh, most men cannot afford more than one, however.

A Bangladeshi family peers through the window of their home.

Approximately 16 percent of Bangladeshis are Hindus. Most of the country's Hindus live in Khulna, Jessore, Dinajpur, Faridpur, and Barisal.

Hindus believe that the soul never dies. Instead, Hindus believe that when people die, they are reborn with their

Hindus in Bangladesh bathe in a river as part of a spiritual cleansing.

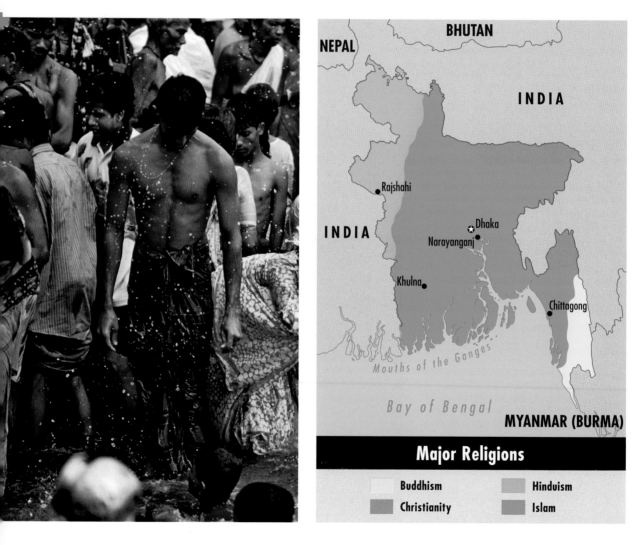

NEPAL

BHUTAN

INDIA

INDIA

Rajshahi

Dhaka

Narayanganj

Khulna

Chittagong

Mouths of the Ganges

Bay of Bengal

MYANMAR (BURMA)

Major Religions

Buddhism   Hinduism

Christianity   Islam

souls in another body. This is called reincarnation. According to the Hindu idea of karma, how people behave in one life affects their condition in the next. It can even affect which caste, or group, a person is born into. The caste system is a basic part of Hinduism.

Bangladeshi Hindus pray during Durga Puja. There are more than 850 million Hindus throughout the world, though most live in India.

It divides people into different groups that determine their lifestyle, behavior, customs, and jobs. In Bangladesh, there are only low- and middle-caste Hindus.

Hindus worship many gods and goddesses, including Shiva, Krishna, Vishnu, and the creator god, Brahma. People

Major Hindu Holy Days

Saraswati Puja
For this holy day, clay statues of Saraswati, the goddess of knowledge, are made.

Holi/Festival of Flowers
At this festival celebrating the end of winter, people dance in the streets and throw colored water at each other.

Rath Jatra
This festival celebrates Jagannath, the lord of the universe.

Durga Puja
This four-day festival honors the mighty warrior goddess Durga.

Diwali/Festival of Lights
This five-day festival celebrates the victory of good over evil. Lamps are lit as a sign of hope.

often worship at shrines in their homes. They also worship in temples. Hindus are tolerant of other religions. They believe that people who follow other religions are simply taking a different path to the same goal.

A Look at Buddhism

Most Buddhists in Bangladesh belong to the tribal communities of the Chittagong Hill Tracts. Buddhism dates back to 500 B.C., when an Indian prince named Siddhartha Gautama set out in search of wisdom. He wandered for six

years trying to find out why people experienced so much sadness in their lives. During periods of intense meditation, he discovered some answers in what came to be known as his Enlightenment. After achieving Enlightenment, Siddhartha was transformed into the Buddha.

He spent the rest of his life teaching the Four Noble Truths to others. These truths are that all lives are filled with suffering; that suffering comes from a desire for worldly things; that suffering ends when desire ends; and that people can learn to escape desire by following the rules of Buddhism. The Buddha taught that if people followed these simple principles, they would reach Nirvana, or a complete release from any suffering.

Sports and Arts

BANGLADESH IS A POOR COUNTRY, BUT IT IS RICH IN ART, culture, and beauty. Bangladeshis love to be entertained and will save up for a long time to buy theater or movie tickets. Less than 7 percent of people in the city and 1 percent of people in the country own their own televisions, so Bangladeshis typically gather together to watch television. Soccer and cricket matches are among the most popular shows.

Opposite: **The Sadarbari Rajbari Folk Art Museum is in Sonargaon.**

Bangladeshis gather to watch television.

Keep an Eye on the Ball

Soccer (called football in Bangladesh) is the favorite sport in the country. Bangladeshis keep up on the scores of their favorite teams. And whenever children find an empty spot and a ball, they are off to play their own soccer games.

Cricket, a ball-and-bat sport that was brought to Bengal by the British, is the nation's second-favorite sport. The Bangladesh national cricket team competes against other nations' teams.

Bangladesh's Tushar Imran hits the ball during a cricket match against Australia.

A Rising Star in Cricket

Born in 1984, Mohammad Ashraful is one of Bangladesh's most famous cricketers. In 2004, Ashraful scored 114 runs against an Indian team and set a new record for the highest individual score of any Bangladeshi. He is considered one of the most promising cricket players in Bangladesh history.

The National Sport

Bangladesh's national sport requires quick moves, long arms, and strong lungs! Called *kabaddi*, the game consists of two teams, each with twelve players. Seven players from each team are on the court at once, while the others are held back until needed.

The court is large, measuring 41 feet by 33 feet (12.5 m by 10 m). It is divided into two halves. The team that wins a coin toss gets to begin. They send a "raider" into the opponent's court. His job is tricky. He has to take

A crowd watches as men play kabaddi.

a deep breath and yell "kabaddi-kabaddi" as he enters the court. His goal is to touch as many players as he can before he takes another gulp of air. Anyone he touches is out. Of course, while he is trying to touch people, the opposing team is trying to hold on to him until he runs out of breath. As soon as he takes another breath, he is out. If he fails to touch anyone during that first deep breath, he is also out. Teams alternate sending a raider to the other side until one team is out of players.

Like Father, Like Son

Rabindranath Tagore had a head start in becoming a poet and philosopher. As the son of a Hindu philosopher and author, it is not surprising that he became an important writer. During his lifetime, he wrote a thousand poems, twenty-four plays, two thousand songs, eight novels, and eight collections of short stories. He also wrote countless articles on social, religious, and political topics. In 1913, he won the Nobel Prize in Literature, the world's most famous literary prize. In this poem, his passion for freedom and his country is clear.

"Where the Mind Is Without Fear"
Where the mind is without fear and the head is held high
Where knowledge is free
Where the world has not been broken up into fragments
By narrow domestic walls
Where words come out from the depth of truth
Where tireless striving stretches its arms towards perfection
Where the clear stream of reason has not lost its way
Into the dreary desert sand of dead habit
Where the mind is led forward by thee
Into ever-widening thought and action
Into that heaven of freedom, our Father, let my country awake.

Festivals often feature traditional folk dance performances.

Drama and Music

Since so many Bangladeshis cannot read, the oral tradition plays a large role in the country's art. Eager crowds love to watch storytellers, singers of folk ballads, and dramas based on romantic legends and mythical figures.

During local festivals, many people enjoy watching *jatras*, or folk dramas, performed onstage. Players act out myths and folklore dating back hundreds of years. They usually use a very exaggerated acting style. Famous folk dances such as *dhali* and *Manipuri* also tell stories.

The Bauls of Bengal

One of the most popular musical groups to come out of Bangladesh is the Bauls of Bengal. The word *baul* means "wind," and just as the wind never stops moving, so this group is determined to never stop wandering from village to village to share their music. They are based on a long tradition of baul musicians.

The group has four members: Narayan Chandra Adhijary, Ramakrishna das Baul, Pabitra Lohar, and Aloy Ghosal. They write and sing their own songs. They also play traditional instruments. These include the *extara*, which has only one string. Another string instrument, the *dotara*, has a long neck and four to seven strings. The *khamak* is a drum with a string around it that is plucked. The Bauls also use percussion instruments such as the *dugi*, a drum made from a small clay pot; a *korotal*, a pair of Indian cymbals; and *gungur* or *nupur*, ankle bells.

As the Bauls of Bengal travel, they carry only what they require. They refuse gifts, taking only food when needed. The men wear simple clothes made from cotton. Their beliefs guide both their personal lifestyles and their music.

Concerts are always popular. Traditional instruments include sitars, violins, bamboo flutes, and drums with names like the *bais, tabla,* and *dhole.* Another common instrument is called the *esraj.* It is like a cross between a cello and a violin, with a short chamber; a long, wide neck; and four strings that are played with a bow. The base of the esraj goes in the musician's lap, while the neck rests on the left shoulder.

Tabla is a pair of drums. The smaller drum is made of wood, while the larger one is usually metal.

Time to Relax

Although few Bangladeshis can afford to go to museums, the country has a large number of them. Dhaka alone has almost two dozen, ranging from the Bangladesh National Museum and the Museum of Science and Technology to the Children's Museum and the Police Museum.

Many Bangladeshis prefer to spend their free time at the local park. They listen to music; drink hot, sweet, milky tea; and watch their children fly kites and play.

Concorde Heritage Park features a scale model of Kantanagar Temple and many other national monuments.

Getting Married

Marriage is an important celebration in Bangladesh. Women wear their prettiest clothes, men put on suits, and everyone gathers to celebrate.

Most marriages in Bangladesh are arranged by parents. Often the groom is much older than the bride, who may be a teenager.

The marriage includes many different events. The first is the *gae halud*. It is similar to the American tradition of a bridal shower, except it involves both the bride and the groom, though separately. The first party is for the bride. Her friends bring her gifts of clothing, jewelry, and sweets. The wife-to-be receives the presents while sitting on a decorated throne. Her mother ties a golden fringed bracelet on her daughter's wrist. Later, each guest puts a dot of the golden spice turmeric on the bride's face and on her own to signify unity. The groom's party is similar.

The next event is the *akht*. Here the bride and groom exchange vows, making an official declaration of marriage. The woman accepts by repeating the word *kobul* three times. The two eat a date, and the ritual is over.

Next comes the *mala badol*. The couple exchanges garlands to symbolize their union. They put a piece of muslin cloth over their heads and share a spicy yogurt drink while looking at each other's reflection in a mirror.

At last comes the *bou bhat*. This is like a wedding reception and is generally hosted by the groom's family. It is the couple's first social activity as husband and wife.

A Day in the Life

LIFE IN BANGLADESH IS FILLED WITH STRUGGLE AND sacrifice. But rather than dwell on the struggle, most Bangladeshis focus on the importance of being together as a family and working the land. When holidays and celebrations come along, they enjoy every moment.

Opposite: **Bangladeshi children often help tend animals and work the land.**

Bangladeshis revel during a parade celebrating the New Year.

Time to Celebrate

Most Bangladeshi holidays focus on religion. The few that do not include:

February 21	Shaheed Dibosh (Martyr's Day)
March 26	Independence Day
April 14	Bengali New Year
May 1	May Day
November 7	National Solidarity/National Revolution Day
December 16	Bijoy Dibosh (Victory Day)
December 26	Boxing Day
December 31	Banking Holiday

Rice is a staple in Bangladesh and throughout South Asia.

In Bangladesh, almost every meal centers on two ingredients: rice and tea. Rice is used in main dishes, side dishes, drinks, and desserts. To add variety, cooks spice the rice with cloves, coriander, cumin, turmeric, and cinnamon. They also boil and fry the rice and add different kinds of meat and fish. Tea, which is called *cha*, is served hot with sugar and milk.

Lentils are the main ingredient of daal.

Bangladeshis usually eat breakfast just after the men return from dawn prayer. It typically consists of hot tea, rice, and perhaps fruit such as mandarin oranges or wild limes. Sometimes women also prepare *chappati*, a round flatbread.

Lunch is the largest meal of the day. Typical dishes include *korma*, a mildly spicy curry with meat and yogurt sauce, and *daal*, a thick soup made of lentils, onions, tomatoes, and spices like garlic and cilantro. Lunch might come with a rich drink called *sandesh*, made from rice, milk, sugar, nuts, and cardamom; or *lassi*, a drink made from yogurt.

Time for Some Rice!

Rice comes in many different varieties. Basmati rice is popular in Bangladesh. While basmati rice cooks, it has a rich smell. Here is a recipe using basmati rice.

Ingredients

1 cup basmati rice

1 small onion

3 medium carrots

1 tablespoon light vegetable oil

1 bay leaf

1 cinnamon stick, crumbled

2 cloves

4 black peppercorns

¼ teaspoon cumin seeds

2 tablespoons butter

1 tablespoon salt

Directions

Wash the rice in cool water until the water runs clear. Put the rice in 2 cups of cool water to soak for 20 minutes. Strain the rice water into an ovenproof saucepan and heat. Leave the rice to dry in a strainer. Preheat the oven to 350°F. While the rice is drying, chop the onion and dice the carrots and set them aside.

When the rice is dry, heat the oil in a heavy skillet. Add the bay leaf, cinnamon, cloves, peppercorns, and cumin. When the spices become fragrant, add the butter and onions. Cook until onions are tender and light golden brown. Add the carrots and cook for 3 to 5 minutes. Add the rice and cook for 5 more minutes, stirring gently. Add the salt and the heated rice water and bring to a boil. Reduce heat and simmer until the water on top of the rice has boiled off.

Cover tightly and bake in the oven for 20 minutes. Remove from the oven, let cool for 10 minutes, and serve.

Dinner is usually served quite late, between 9:30 and 10:00 at night. All meals are eaten while sitting on the floor. People pick up the food with their fingers rather than silverware.

Bangladesh has few restaurants except in the biggest cities. Most people eat at home or buy snacks from street vendors. Cooking is considered women's work, and girls are taught how to cook at a young age.

Bangladeshis buy snacks sold by a street vendor.

Bangladeshi kitchens are simple. The stoves are usually built right into the mud floor, and the most common utensils are grinding stones, earthenware pots, and handmade baskets. Some of the cooking is done outside in a communal area.

Women prepare a meal using simple stoves.

Welcoming a New Life

Because Bangladesh has few doctors, hospitals, or medical centers, many babies are born at home. The mother gives birth with only female friends and family to help. Even midwives are too expensive for most families. Baby boys are almost always preferred over baby girls.

When a woman goes into labor, she and the other women retreat to a birthing room. They stay there for the entire birth process. The new mother and baby remain in the room for nine days, only coming out to use the bathroom. Even then, they must have another woman with them and carry a curved blade or a burning stick to ward off the evil spirits that men fear they will attract. Some families also try to deflect evil spirits by putting a charm around the baby's waist or soot on the soles of the feet, on the forehead, and around the eyes.

When the nine days are over, the mother and baby are bathed in a ritual bath. The birthing room is swept and cleaned thoroughly, and the used linens are boiled to sterilize them. The woman and her baby then return to the room for another month. When they finally emerge, the room is once again cleaned and the linens sterilized.

The central courtyard is generally thought of as the women's area. In fact, most men are not allowed to enter it without permission. The *kanta*, a garden area at the rear of the house, is also off-limits to men. It is where vegetables and fruits are grown and where the water pump is located. It is typically the area where the women bathe, as well.

Keeping Cool

When it comes to clothing in Bangladesh, the most important thing is keeping cool. The constant heat and humidity make light, loose outfits the rule. The particular style worn, however, sometimes depends on a person's religion.

Most Muslim men wear a *lungi*, a patterned piece of cloth that wraps around the waist. On top, they wear a Western-style shirt. Hindu men, on the other hand, commonly wear a

Burying the Dead

In Muslim families, after a person dies, the body is washed and carefully wrapped in a muslin cloth. It is then buried, often on the same day as the death.

A Hindu farmer wearing a dhoti harvests rice.

dhoti, a long piece of cloth that wraps around the waist and between the legs. Some wear a Punjabi suit made of white cotton. It has loose pants and a shirt with long tails. Some men wear *nagra*, traditional decorated slippers. Others go barefoot or wear light sandals.

Women's clothing can be much more elaborate. Some women wear colorful saris. Saris are made from pieces of cloth 18 feet (5.5 m) long. The cloth wraps around the waist to form a skirt and then drapes over one shoulder. A short blouse is worn underneath. Cotton saris are worn during the week, while silk ones are reserved for special occasions.

Some women also wear *shalwar kameez,* a long, loose top that goes to the knees. Loose pants are worn underneath. If it is cool out, some women add a *dupata*, a decorative shawl that covers the head.

Saris are often brightly colored and patterned.

Getting Around

Few people in Bangladesh own their own cars. Even if they did, the rain and floods would make them unusable for a good part of the year.

In a land where it sometimes seems there are more waterways than roads, it is no surprise that boats are one of the best ways to get around. The rivers in Bangladesh are usually full of all kinds of watercraft. Some people use canoes. Others have

Boats wait to ferry passengers from a dock in Dhaka.

Boats loaded with wood leave the Sundarbans.

"country boats," small boats that are paddled or pushed by a pole. They are used for everything from moving people from one village to another to taking jute bundles to mills downstream. During the rainy season, these boats are busier than ever since many roads are under water and bridges may have been washed away.

Steamers crowded with passengers prepare to leave Dhaka.

Large oceangoing vessels ply the largest rivers. Other large boats in Bangladesh include ferryboats and steamers. These are used for longer trips and heavier loads. They do not move fast, often taking as long as three days to travel 250 miles (400 km). In recent years, they have proven to be quite dangerous as well. The country has no strict regulations on how many people can climb aboard. Between 2002 and 2005, at least seven of these ferries sank, causing the deaths of nearly nine hundred people.

While many Bangladeshi boats are slow, three-wheeled bicycle rickshaws zip around. With its padded seat, retractable hood, and comfortable footrests, the rickshaw is a preferred method of moving around in cities. Rickshaws zigzag through the bumper-to-bumper traffic. Although they are supposed to be registered, most of them are not. Experts estimate that at least 180,000 of these brightly colored vehicles weave through the streets of Bangladesh.

Rickshaws speed through city streets.

The first rickshaw came to Bangladesh in 1938. It arrived on a boat from Calcutta, India. It did not take long for people to realize that rickshaws were a useful mode of transportation—and a way to make money. Rickshaws have many advantages. They are pollution-free, quiet, and inexpensive. But they also have been known to cause traffic accidents when their drivers dart in front of cars. The risk of injury to rickshaw drivers is high.

The life of a rickshaw driver is not easy. It is hard work pedaling people and heavy cargo around busy streets for at least ten hours every day. Many drivers take pride in their work, however, often decorating their rickshaws with bright paintings, plastic flowers, streamers, and bells. When a Bangladeshi raises his arm, waves, and says "*Khali,*" rickshaw drivers head straight for him. Sometimes, drivers compete for the same customer. They will each ring their bell, but they all know that the first driver to get there wins.

Timeline

Bangladesh History

The Bang people settle in what is now Bangladesh.	About 1000 B.C.
The Mauryan Empire rules the area.	273–232 B.C.
Gopala founds the Pala dynasty, bringing Buddhism to Bengal.	A.D. 750
The Senas bring Hinduism to the region.	1150
Muslims take control of Bengal, establishing the Delhi Sultanate.	1206
Bengal falls under the control of the Mughal Empire.	1576
Dhaka becomes the capital of the Mughal Empire's Bengal Province.	1608
The British begin arriving in Bengal.	1650
The East India Company gains control of Bengal.	1757
Famine kills 30 percent of Bengal's population.	1769

World History

2500 B.C.	Egyptians build the pyramids and the Sphinx in Giza.
563 B.C.	The Buddha is born in India.
A.D. 313	The Roman emperor Constantine legalizes Christianity.
610	The Prophet Muhammad begins preaching a new religion called Islam.
1054	The Eastern (Orthodox) and Western (Roman) Catholic Churches break apart.
1095	The Crusades begin.
1215	King John seals the Magna Carta.
1300s	The Renaissance begins in Italy.
1347	The plague sweeps through Europe.
1453	Ottoman Turks capture Constantinople, conquering the Byzantine Empire.
1492	Columbus arrives in North America.
1500s	Reformers break away from the Catholic Church, and Protestantism is born.
1776	The Declaration of Independence is signed.
1789	The French Revolution begins.

Bangladesh History

People rise up against the East India Company in the Indian Rebellion.	1857
The East India Company is dissolved, and the British Raj begins.	1858
Bengal is divided into East Bengal and West Bengal.	1905–1911
India and Pakistan gain their independence.	1947
Police kill student demonstrators in Dhaka during the Language Movement.	1952
East Bengal is renamed East Pakistan.	1955
The Bhola Cyclone kills hundreds of thousands of people; the Awami League, which supports Bangladeshi independence, wins national elections.	1970
Civil war breaks out; Bangladesh becomes independent.	1971
Mujibur Rahman becomes prime minister.	1972
Rahman is assassinated.	1975
Hussain Muhammad Ershad takes control of the country in a coup.	1982
Ershad is forced out of office.	1990
Begum Khaleda Zia becomes Bangladesh's first female prime minister; the Bangladesh Cyclone kills 139,000 people.	1991
Sheikh Hasina Wajed becomes prime minister.	1996
Khaleda Zia again becomes prime minister.	2001

World History

1865	The American Civil War ends.
1879	The first practical light bulb is invented.
1914	World War I breaks out.
1917	The Bolshevik Revolution brings communism to Russia.
1929	A worldwide economic depression begins.
1939	World War II begins.
1945	World War II ends.
1957	The Vietnam War starts.
1969	Humans land on the Moon.
1975	The Vietnam War ends.
1989	The Berlin Wall is torn down as communism crumbles in Eastern Europe.
1991	The Soviet Union breaks into separate states.
2001	Terrorists attack the World Trade Center, New York, and the Pentagon, Washington, D.C.

Fast Facts

Official name: People's Republic of Bangladesh

Capital: Dhaka

Official language: Bangla

Khulna

BANGLADESH
- Cities of over 200,000 people
- Other cities
- National capital

0   80 miles

0   80 kilometers

BHUTAN

NEPAL

Thakurgaon

Pirgani   Saidpur   Lalmanir Hat

Dinajpur   Rangpur

Brahmaputra River

Bangladesh

Ganges River

Naogaon   Bogra   Jamalpur   Jaria   Chhatak   Sylhet

Nawabganj   Rautpara

Sirajganj   Mymensingh   Gouripur

INDIA   Rajshahi   Ishurdi   Tangail   Habiganj

Kushtia   Pabna   Bhairab Bazaar

Chuadanga   Dhaka   Brahmanbaria   INDIA

Faridpur   Narayanganj

Munshiganj   Comilla

Jessore   Chandpur   Laksham

Madaripur   Meghna R.   Noakhali   Khagrachari

Khulna   Barisal   Bhola   Nazir   Rangamati
Hat
Bagerhat   Chandraghona
Bandarban
Patuakhali   Chittagong

Sundarbans   Satkania   Bichari
National Park

Mouths of the Ganges   Cox's Bazaar

Bay of Bengal   MYANMAR
(BURMA)

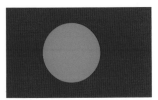

Bangladesh's flag

Official religion:	Islam
Year of founding:	1971
National anthem:	"Amar Shonar Bangia" ("My Golden Bengal")
Type of government:	Parliamentary democracy
Chief of state:	President
Head of government:	Prime minister
Area:	55,584 square miles (143,962 sq km)
Latitude and longitude of geographic center:	24°00'N, 90°00'E
Bordering countries:	India and Myanmar
Highest elevation:	Mount Keokradong, 4,035 feet (1,230 m) above sea level
Lowest elevation:	Sea level, along the Indian Ocean
Average temperatures in Dhaka:	90°F (32°C), in summer and 67°F (19°C) in winter
Average annual precipitation:	55 to 235 inches (140 cm to 600 cm)
National population:	147,365,352

Royal Bengal tiger

Mohasthangarh

Currency

Population of largest cities (2003 est):

Dhaka	18.7 million
Chittagong	5 million
Khulna	2.4 million

Famous landmarks:

▶ *National Martyr's Monument*, Dhaka

▶ *Dhaka Zoo*, Dhaka

▶ *Mohasthangarh*, Bogra

▶ *Cox's Bazaar*, coastline

▶ *Foy's Lake*, Chittagong

Industry: Bangladesh is primarily agricultural; its main crops are rice, jute, and tea. The garment-export industry is on the rise, as are the fishing industry and leather production. Traditional crafts, such as terra-cotta pottery and woven straw and bamboo, are growing industries as well.

Currency: The taka. In 2006, US$1 equaled 69.45 takas.

Weights and measures: Metric system

Literacy rate: 43 percent

Schoolchildren

Muhammad Yunus

Common Bangla words and phrases:

Asalaam alaykum	Hello (to a Muslim)
Nomaashkaar	Hello (to a Hindu)
Khudaa hafiz	Good-bye
Pore dakhaa hobe	See you later
Maaf korun	Excuse me
Ji	Yes
Naa	No
Tik aache	No Problem
Kaamon aachen?	How are you?
Bhaalo aahi	I'm fine
Aapnaar naam ki?	What's your name?
Aami bujhi naa	I don't understand
Aami jaabo . . .	I want to go to . . .
Kotaai . . . ?	Where is . . . ?
Koto dur . . . ?	How far is . . . ?

Famous Bangladeshis:

Aroj Ali Matubbar   (1900–1985)
Philospher

Mujibur Rahman   (1920–1975)
The father of Bangladeshi independence

Rabindranath Tagore   (1861–1941)
Nobel Prize–winning poet

Sheikh Hasina Wajed   (1947–)
Former prime minister

Muhammad Yunus   (1940–)
Founder of the Grameen Bank Project

Begum Khaleda Zia   (1945–)
First female prime minister

To Find Out More

Books

▶ Khoo, Eileen. *Welcome to Bangladesh.* Milwaukee, Wis.: Gareth Stevens, 2005.

▶ Lewin, Ted. *Sacred River: The Ganges of India.* New York: Clarion Books, 2003.

▶ London, Ellen. *Bangladesh.* Milwaukee, Wis.: Gareth Stevens, 2004.

▶ Montgomery, Sy. *The Man-Eating Tigers of Sundarbans.* Boston: Houghton-Mifflin, 2001

▶ Valliant, Doris. *Bangladesh.* Philadelphia: Mason Crest, 2005.

Web Sites

▶ **Virtual Bangladesh**
http://www.virtualbangladesh.com
To find a wide array of information on topics such as history, food, and animals.

▶ **Visit Bangladesh Lonely Planet**
http://www.lonelyplanet.com/ worldguide/destinations/asia/ bangladesh
For basic information useful to travelers.

▶ **The World Factbook: Bangladesh**
http://www.cia.gov/cia/publications/ factbook/geos/bg.html
For all kinds of basic information about Bangladesh.

Organizations and Embassies

▶ **Bangladesh Embassy**
3510 International Drive NW,
Suite 300–325
Washington, DC 20008
202-342-8372
http://www.bangladoot.org

▶ **High Commission for Bangladesh**
275 Bank Street, Suite 302
Ottawa, Ontario K2P 2L6
613-236-0138
http://www.bdhc.org

▶ **Permanent Mission of Bangladesh
to the United Nations**
227 E. 45th Street, 14th floor
New York, NY 10017
212-867-3434
http://www.un.int/bangladesh

Index

Page numbers in *italics* indicate illustrations.

Meet the Author

TAMRA ORR is a full-time writer and author living in the Pacific Northwest. She has written many books for the Enchantment of the World series, including *Slovenia, Indonesia,* and *Turkey.* She is also the author of the award-winning *School Violence: Halls of Hope, Halls of Fear,* as well as *America's Best Colleges for B Students* and *When the Mirror Lies: Anorexia, Bulimia, and Other Eating Disorders.*

Orr graduated from Ball State University in 1982 with a degree in English and secondary education. She is mother to four and life partner to Joseph. In addition to writing books, Orr writes educational assessment material and magazine articles.

To Orr, researching a book or article is one of the best ways of finding out about the world. To find out more about Bangladesh, she visited libraries and scoured online bookstores to find material that might provide valuable information. She contacted international organizations and spent endless hours on the Internet. Orr also listened to the recording of the 1971 benefit concert for Bangladesh for the first time. She even gave a few Bangladeshi recipes a try!

Orr relishes the chance to explore a whole new country. Even more, she loves sharing what she has learned with her family, who have to listen—she will test them on it!

Photo Credits